TO: ~~Connie~~

FROM: ~~Diana~~

DATE: ~~1/29/14~~

May you always have work for your hands to do.
May your pockets hold always a coin or two.
May the sun shine bright on your windowpane.
May the rainbow be certain to follow each rain.
May the hand of a friend always be near you.
And may God fill your heart with gladness to cheer you.

IRISH BLESSINGS

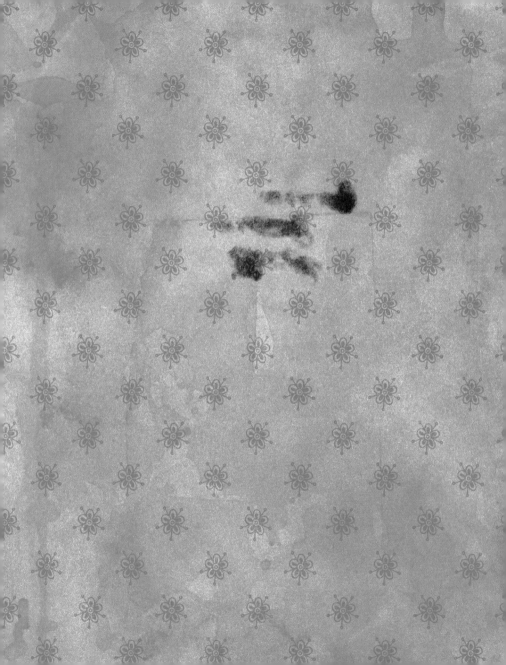

BLESSED TO CALL YOU FrienD

HARVEST HOUSE PUBLISHERS
EUGENE, OREGON

ARTWORK BY
ANNIE LAPOINT

To my daughter Joanna, who demonstrates true grace, beauty, and joy. I am so grateful for the time, the laughter, and the fun we have together. I am blessed to call you friend!

—*Momma*

BLESSED TO CALL YOU FRIEND

Text copyright © 2014 by Harvest House Publishers
Artwork copyright © by Annie LaPoint

Published by Harvest House Publishers
Eugene, Oregon 97402
www.harvesthousepublishers.com

ISBN 978-0-7369-6218-6

All artwork is copyrighted by Annie LaPoint. License granted by Penny Lane Publishing, Inc.®. For more information regarding artwork featured in this book, please contact Penny Lane Publishing at info@pennylanepublishing.com.

Design and production by Dugan Design Group, Bloomington, Minnesota

Harvest House Publishers has made every effort to trace the ownership of all poems and quotes. In the event of a question arising from the use of a poem or quote, we regret any error made and will be pleased to make the necessary correction in future editions of this book.

All Scripture verses are taken from the Holy Bible, New International Version®, NIV®. Copyright © 1973, 1978, 1984, 2011 by Biblica, Inc.® Used by permission. All rights reserved worldwide.

Printed in China

14 15 16 17 18 19 20 21 / LP / 10 9 8 7 6 5 4 3 2 1

Dear friend, I am so grateful for all the
blessings you give to me by being you.
The greatest blessing of all is your friendship.

CONTENTS

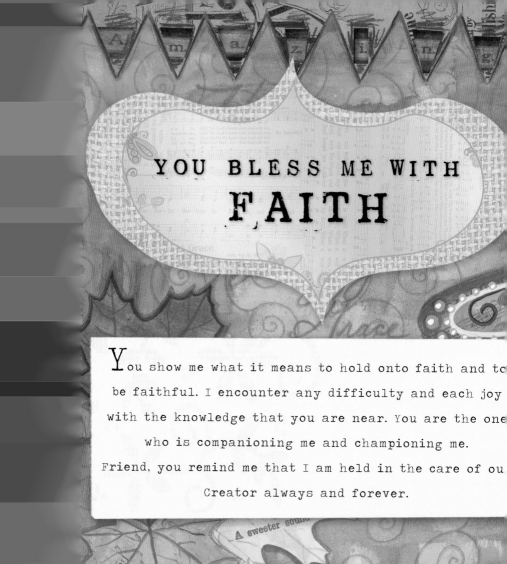

YOU BLESS ME WITH
FAITH

You show me what it means to hold onto faith and to be faithful. I encounter any difficulty and each joy with the knowledge that you are near. You are the one who is companioning me and championing me. Friend, you remind me that I am held in the care of our Creator always and forever.

A sweeter sound

Psalm 75:1

Gra

No. 251.
John Newton

Amazing

Dear friends, let us love one another, for love comes from God.

I JOHN 4:7

5

Of all the best things upon earth, I hold that a faithful friend is the best.
OWEN MEREDITH

Those blessings are sweetest that are won with prayer and worn with thanks.
HOMAS GOODWIN

praise

l lead us home

A true friend is the gift of God, and he only who made hearts can unite them.

ROBERT SOUTH

A life of prayer is a life whose litanies are ever fresh acts of self-devoting love.

FREDERICK WILLIAM ROBERTSON

Friendship is the holiest of gifts,
God can bestow nothing more sacred upon us!
It enhances every joy, mitigates every pain.
Everyone can have a friend
Who himself knows how to be a friend.

CHRISTOPH AUGUST TIEDGE

The most I can do for my friend is simply to be his friend.
I have no wealth to bestow on him. If he knows that I am happy
in loving him, he will want no other reward.
Is not friendship divine in this?

HENRY DAVID THOREAU

FAITH

Faith is the root of all blessings.
JEREMY TAYLOR

It is good for us to think no grace or blessing truly ours till we are aware that God has blessed some one else with it through us.

PHILLIPS BROOKS

For All I Trust Him

Faith

Friendship

YOU BLESS ME WITH
RENEWAL

Whether we share a morning in a café chatting or a moment in deep silence pondering, my spirit is refreshed. I love how we bond over everything from the silly to the substantial. You restore my belief in goodness and possibility. My life is enriched because you are an ever-present source of renewal and hope.

trust

When thou has truly thanked the Lord for every blessing sent, But little time will then remain for murmur or lament.

HANNAH MOORE

To remain young
while growing old is the
highest blessing.
GERMAN PROVERB

Live
It
Fully
Everyday

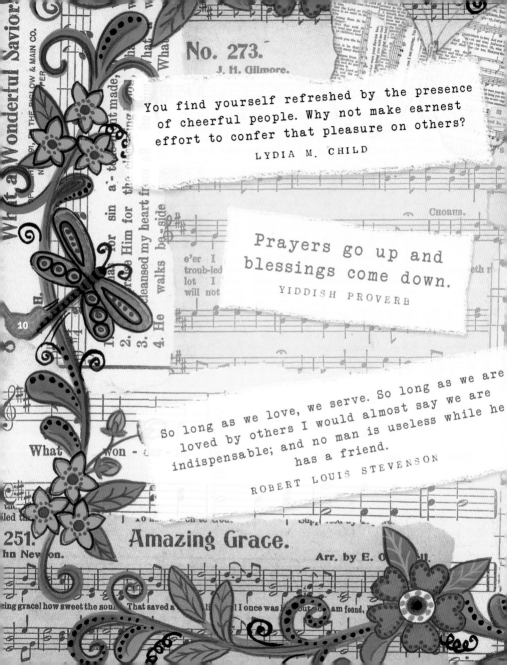

No. 273.
J. H. Gilmore.

You find yourself refreshed by the presence of cheerful people. Why not make earnest effort to confer that pleasure on others?

LYDIA M. CHILD

Prayers go up and blessings come down.

YIDDISH PROVERB

So long as we love, we serve. So long as we are loved by others I would almost say we are indispensable; and no man is useless while he has a friend.

ROBERT LOUIS STEVENSON

251.
hn Newton.

Amazing Grace.

Arr. by E. O.

Perfume and incense bring joy to the heart,
and the pleasantness of one's friend springs
from his earnest counsel.

PROVERBS 27:9

Gratitude bestows reverence...changing forever
how we experience life and the world.

JOHN MILTON

There is nothing like putting the shine on
another's face to put the shine on our own.

WILLIAM CHANNING GANNETT

We live in deeds, not
years; in thoughts,
not breaths.

PHILIP JAMES BAILEY

YOU BLESS ME WITH
INSIGHT

So many times you have invited me to cast my eyes on a silver lining, a forgotten joy, or the exquisiteness of a garden flower. When I am stuck in a rut, you reach out to me with a new perspective and lift me above my circumstances. Thank you for sharing with me the lens of grace—through it I witness the beauty that brightens my days.

We may scatter the seeds of courtesy and kindness about us at little expense. Some of them will fall on good ground, and grow up into benevolence in the minds of others, and all of them will bear fruit of happiness in the bosom whence they spring. Once blest are all the virtues; twice blest, sometimes.

THOMAS BENTHAM

Come sound His praise a - broad

Always look
out for the
sunlight the
Lord sends into
your days.
HOPE CAMPBELL

Send me your
light and your
faithful care,
let them lead me;
let them bring
me to your
holy mountain,
to the place
where you dwell.
PSALM 43:3

13

Prayer

Changes

Everything

One of the most beautiful qualities
of true friendship is to understand and
to be understood.
LUCIUS SENECA

A word of
kindness is seldom
spoken in vain.
GEORGE D. PRENTICE

A true friend...advises justly, assists readily, adventures boldly, takes all
patiently, defends courageously, and continues a friend unchangeably.

WILLIAM PENN

An honest heart being the
first blessing, a knowing
head is the second.
THOMAS JEFFERSON

Never undertake anything for which you
wouldn't have the courage to ask the
blessings of heaven.

GEORG LICHTENBERG

Our prayers should be for blessings in general,
for God knows best what is good for us.
SOCRATES

INSIGHT

Be WISE

and keep your heart on the right path.
Proverbs 23:19

YOU BLESS ME WITH
ENCOURAGEMENT

I have aspirations that have come true because you are the cheerleader in my life. Your notes, words, and prayers buoy my spirits and bolster my resolve. Is there nothing I can't do with your support? I don't sin into my insecurities anymore; instead, I stand upon your blessing of encouragement. I send up cheers for you in all that you endeavor. *Hip hip hooray.*

Two people are better than one, because they have a good return for their labor.

ECCLESIASTES 4:9

~Life Is An~
ADVENTURE

An effort made for the happiness of others lifts above ourselves.

LYDIA M. CHILD

Enjoy
The
Journey

PAINTER
love

N. DAKOTA B 62
91-233
PEACE GARDEN STATE

PARK
35¢
ONE TICKET

17

JUST GO

Blessed are the joymakers. - NATHANIEL PARKER WILLIS

Don't walk in front of me I may not follow. Don't walk behind me, I may not lead. Just walk beside me and be my friend.
ALBERT CAMUS

The faithfulness of the Lord endures forever.
PSALM 117:2

A light heart lives long.
SHAKESPEARE

The most utterly lost of all days, is that in which you have not once laughed.
SEBASTIAN CHAMFORT

Our real blessings often appear to us in the shape of pains, losses and disappointments; but let us have patience and we soon shall see them in proper figures.

JOSEPH ADDISON

Friends...they cherish each other's hopes. They are kind to each other's dreams.

HENRY DAVID THOREAU

Friendship

YOU BLESS ME WITH
NOURISHMENT

Kindness born of your heart nourishes my heart.

I love how we can laugh and cry together.

When that happens, I believe it feeds and waters the

seeds of friendship we have planted over the years.

We are growing a beautiful garden, you and I!

Blessed is the influence of one true, loving human soul on another. - George Eliot

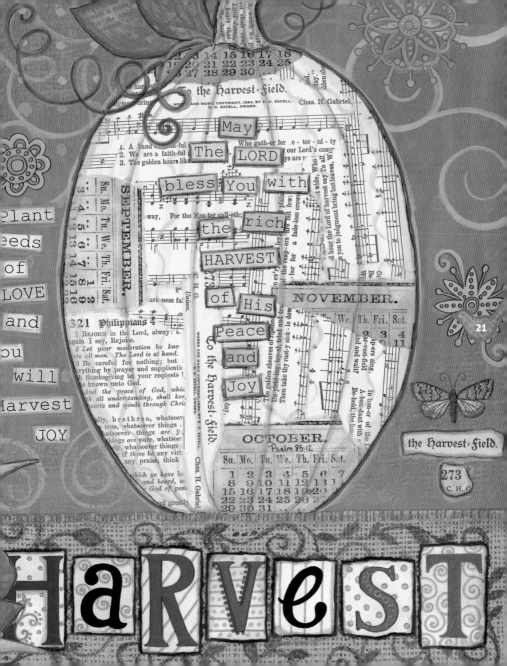

I could not live without the love of my friends

JOHN KEATS

Friendships are fragile things,
and require as much care in
handling as any other fragile
and precious thing.

RANDOLPH S. BOURNE

But friendship is precious, not only in the shad
but in the sunshine of life; and thanks to a
benevolent arrangement of things, the greate
part of life is sunshine.

THOMAS JEFFERSON

I have always preferred the sunshine and
have tried to put other people there,
if only for an hour or two at a time.

MARSHALL P. WILDER

God appoints our graces to be nurses to other men's weaknesses.

HENRY WARD BEECHER

Friendship does not spring
up and grow great and
become perfect all at once,
but requires time and the
nourishment of thoughts.

DANTE

N O U R I S H M E N T

Words cannot express the joy which a friend imparts; they only can know who have experienced. A friend is dearer than the light of heaven, for it would be better for us that the sun were extinguished than that we should be without friends.

SAINT JOHN CHRYSOSTOM

May every soul that touches mine—
Be it the slightest contact—
Get there from some good;
Some little grace; one kindly thought;
One aspiration yet unfelt;
One bit of courage
For the darkening sky;
One gleam of faith
To brave the thickening ills of life;
One glimpse of brighter skies
Beyond the gathering mists—
To make this life worth while.

GEORGE ELIOT

Let us be grateful to people who make us happy; they are the charming gardeners who make our souls blossom.

MARCEL PROUST

YOU BLESS ME WITH
DELIGHT

Would I laugh out loud if you were not in my life? I pray I never have to find out the answer to that question. Your good-hearted nature is a gift I treasure. You show me how to look on the bright side, and then you grab my hand and help me walk in the light of new joy.

Next to a good soul-stirring prayer is a good laugh.
SAMUEL MUTCHMORE

It is a friendly heart that has plenty of friends.
WILLIAM THACKERAY

THIS
IS
MY
FATHER'S
WORLD

HOME

CHooSe to Be HappY

Joy is more divine than sorrow, for joy is
bread and sorrow is medicine.

HENRY WARD BEECHER

The laughter of girls is, and ever was, among the
delightful sounds of earth.

THOMAS DE QUINCEY

I like the laughter that opens the lips and
the heart, that shows at the same time
pearls and the soul.

VICTOR HUGO

While I keep my senses I shall prefer nothing to a pleasant friend.

HORACE

Cheerfulness is the offshoot of goodness.

CHRISTIAN NESTELL BOVEE

Burdens become light when cheerfully borne.

OVID

DELIGHT

a-maz-ing

lovel

Friends

A friend is someone who reaches for your hand but touches your he

EXPLORE

See
The
World

It's Time For An Adventure

To laugh often and much; to win the respect of intelligent people and the affection of children; to earn the appreciation of honest critics and endure the betrayal of false friends; to appreciate beauty, to find the best in others; to leave the world a bit better, whether by a healthy child, a garden patch or a redeemed social condition; to know even one life has breathed easier because you lived. This is to have succeeded.

RALPH WALDO EMERSON

Be Of Good CHeer

Friendship

YOU BLESS ME WITH STRENGTH AND VULNERABILITY

I used to put on my brave face when I approached a challenge. But you saw through it in a heartbeat and reminded me that there's great strength in being vulnerable with those who hold us with respect and tenderness. It is a blessing to be myself with another person. May my presence create a strong and comforting place for the true you to shine.

Two persons cannot long be friends if they cannot forgive each other's little failings.

JEAN DE LA BRUYÈRE

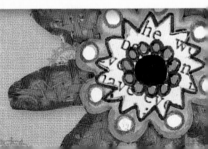

Wondrous is the strength of cheerfulness, and its power of endurance.

THOMAS CARLYLE

Live It Fully Everyday

LifE

30

HOPE

Be true to your work, your word and your friend.
HENRY DAVID THOREAU

I once was lost but now am found

True friendship consists not in the multitude of friends, but in their worth and value.
BEN JONSON

The supreme happiness of life is the conviction of being loved for yourself, or, more correctly, being loved in spite of yourself.
VICTOR HUGO

Oh, the comfort—the inexpressible comfort of feeling safe with a person, Having neither to weigh thoughts, Nor measure words—but pouring them All right out—just as they are— Chaff and grain together— Certain that a faithful hand will Take and sift them— Keep what is worth keeping— And with the breath of kindness Blow the rest away.
DINAH MARIA MULOCK CRAIK

The very society of joy redoubles it; so that, while it lights upon my friend it rebounds upon myself, and the brighter his candle burns the more easily will it light mine.
ROBERT SOUTH

31

Life is made up, not of great sacrifices or duties, but of little things, in which smiles, and kindnesses, and small obligations, given habitually, are what win and preserve the heart and secure comfort.
SIR HUMPHRY DAVY

It is not so much our friends' help that helps us as the confident knowledge that they will help us.
EPICURUS

YOU BLESS ME WITH
HOSPITALITY

Welcome! Your smile speaks this in high volume.
You invite me to the shelter of your friendship with
lavish portions of compassion and attention. I feel at
home wherever you are because you extend your cheer,
talents, praises, and support without any strings
attached—which ties my heart to your graciousness
all the more.

What is a friend? I will tell you. It is a person
with whom you dare to be yourself. - FRANK CRANE

How good
and pleasant it is
when God's people live
together in unity!

PSALM 133:1

LOVE

FaMiLY

are like the branches of a tree growing in different
directions yet our roots will always remain as one

A Friend is someone who reaches f
your hand but touches your he

One who knows how to show and to accept kindness will be a friend better than any possession.
SOPHOCLES

Love is flower-like; Friendship is like a sheltering tree.
SAMUEL TAYLOR COLERIDG

Be yourself, simple, honest, and unpretending, and you will enjoy through life the respect and love of friends.
WILLIAM SHERMAN

A little peaceful home bounds all my wants and wishes; Add to this my book and friend— and this is happiness supreme.
MICHEL DE MONTAIGNE

Better than gold is a peaceful home
Where all the fireside characters come,
The shrine of love, the heaven of life,
Hallowed by mother, or sister, or wife,
However humble the home may be,
Or tried with sorrow by heaven's decree,
The blessings that never were bought or sold
And center there, are better than gold.
ABRAM J. RYAN

The expensiveness of friendship does not lie in what one does for one's friends, but in what, out of regard for them, one leaves undone.
HENRIK IBSEN

First
And
Most
I Love You

His Great Love.

Yes, Jesus loves me
Yes, Jesus loves me
Yes, Jesus loves me

The Bible tells me so.

No. 103.

1. Je - sus loves me!
2. Je - sus loves me!
3. Je - sus loves me!
4. Je - sus loves me!

FaMiLY

All the blessings we enjoy are Divine deposits, committed to our trust on this condition, that they should be dispensed for the benefit of our neighbors.
JOHN CALVIN

Not what we give, but what we share,
For the gift without the giver is bare:
Who gives himself with his alms feeds three,
Himself, his hungering neighbor, and Me.
JAMES RUSSELL LOWELL

Do all the good you can,
By all the means you can,
In all the ways you can,
In all the places you can,
At all the times you can,
To all the people you can,
As long as ever you can.
JOHN WESLEY

There are many locks in my house and all with different keys, but I have one master-key which opens them all. The Lord has many treasures and secrets all shut up from carnal minds with locks which they cannot open. But he who walks in fellowship with Jesus possesses the master-key which will open to him all the blessings of the covenant and even the very heart of God.
CHARLES SPURGEON

YOU BLESS ME WITH
INSPIRATION

You have been by my side when I've taken timid steps, inching my way along a path of discovery. And you are definitely the friend I want to face the future with. In unison, let's breathe in and out, count to three, and take a big leap into the mystery ahead. May we always inspire one another to dream in full color as we awaken to the wonder of lives unfolding.

The love of friendship is the most perfect form of loving.

CARDINAL MANNING

My treasures are my friends.

CONSTANTIUS

My friend peers in on
me with merry
Wise face, and though th
sky stay dim,
The very light of day,
the very
Sun's self comes in with h

ALGERNON SWINBURNE

Laugh if you
are wise.

MARTIAL

Get into the habit of looking for the silver lining of
the cloud, and when you have found it, continue
to look at it, rather than at the leaden gray in the
middle. It will help you over many hard places.

A.A. WILLITTS

Every one must have felt that a
cheerful friend is like a sunny day,
which sheds its brightness on
all around.

SIR JOHN LUBBOCK

It is great to have friends when one is young, but indeed it is still more so when y
are getting old. When we are young, friends are, like everything else, a matter
course. In the old days we know what it means to have them.

EDWARD GRIEG

If instead of a gem, or even a flower, we should cast the gift of a loving
thought into the heart of a friend, that would be giving as the angels give.

GEORGE MACDONALD

INSPIRATION

HOPE

A Joyful Anticipation Of Something Good

Psalm 37:4

I. H. Gilmore.

> A friend may well be reckoned
> the masterpiece of nature.
> RALPH WALDO EMERSON

> The highest wisdom is continual cheerfulness;
> such a state, like the region above the moon,
> is always clear and serene.
> MICHEL MONTAIGNE

> What sunshine is to flowers,
> smiles are to humanity.
> JOSEPH ADDISON

INSPIRATION

Amazing

Grace

YOU BLESS ME WITH
PEACE

My restless heart is given great peace each time I rest in the comfort of our true connection. I never walk alone through my days because you are my friend. You steady me with your grace and calm me with a hand on my shoulder at just the right moment. May you be blessed in full measure for all the ways you make life better for me and so many others.

Speak, move, act in peace as if you were in prayer. In truth, this is prayer.

FRANCIS DE S. FENELO

God is Love

Let the Peace of Christ rule in your hearts Colossians 3:15

As grace is first from God, so it is continually from him, as much as light is all day long from the sun, as well as at first dawn or at sun-rising.

JONATHAN EDWARDS

May good luck be your friend in whatever you do and may trouble be always a stranger to you.

IRISH BLESSING

How truly is a kind heart a fountain of gladness, making everything in its vicinity freshen into smiles.

WASHINGTON IRVING

It hain't no use to grumble and complane;
It's jest as cheap and easy to rejoice.
When God sorts out the weather and sends rain,
W'y, rain's my choice.

JAMES WHITCOMB RILEY

There is indeed no blessing of life that is any way comparable to the enjoyment of a discreet and virtuous friend. It eases and unloads the mind, clears and improves the understanding, engenders thoughts and knowledge, animates virtue and good resolutions, soothes and allays the passions, and finds employment for most of the vacant hours of life.

JOSEPH ADDISON

PEACE

May you have warm words on a
cool evening, a full moon on a
dark night, and a smooth road
all the way to your door.

IRISH SAYING

May God grant you many years to live,
For sure he must be knowing
The earth has angels all too few
And Heaven is overflowing.

IRISH BLESSING

God gave man an upright countenance to survey
the heavens, and to look upward to the stars.

OVID

Lovely concord and most sacred peace doth nourish virtue,
and fast friendship breed.

EDMUND SPENSER

Peace is the evening star of the soul, as virtue is its sun;
and the two are never far apart.

CALEB COLTON

Reflect upon your present blessings—of which every man has many—
not on your past misfortunes, of which all men have some.

CHARLES DICKENS,
A Christmas Carol and other Christmas Writings

I will only add, God bless you.

JANE AUSTEN